Organized Mess

Inspiring Stories of Unwelcome Loss with Encouragement!

Jan Sherman

Copyright 2018 Jan Sherman

ALL RIGHTS RESERVED. This book contains material protected under International and Federal Copyright Laws and Treaties. Any unauthorized reprint or use of this material is prohibited. No part of this book may be reproduced or transmitted in any form or by any means, electronic or mechanical, including photocopying, recording, or by any information storage and retrieval system without express written permission from the author/publisher.

Hardcover
ISBN: 978-1-64184-912-8

Paperback
ISBN: 978-1-64184-913-5

ebook
ISBN: 978-1-64184-914-2

ABOUT THE AUTHOR

After my son, Brandon, passed away unexpectedly at the age of nineteen, I was consistently looking for something or someone to give me a glimmer of encouragement. People were speechless, and they didn't know how to approach me. Do they bring up my son's name? Do they ignore the fact that I just lost my only child? What do they say to me now? So, in every effort to do something, most people did nothing.

Now it's been several years since my son was taken from me, and I find myself asking God to lead me to those that also need encouragement. Those who have been left desolate, or who have lost a loved one, are near and dear to my heart. Losing a child is the most devastating thing that I've been through, yet I find myself still giving God my praise because He is the One who loves me the most, and I realize how my existence solely depends on Him.

My life is a place of joy and laughter as well as a place filled with tears, forgiveness, gratefulness, and love. I am forever thinking of Brandon in almost everything I do. He is a part of my sorrow, but remembering his smile and laughter brings me great joy. Being a single mom early in my motherhood years, I acknowledge and connect with other single moms who are doing the best they can and still struggle a bit. Bringing encouragement to mothers who are hurting, discouraged, and ready to give up is a great honor.

My grandmother had a wonderful relationship with God in a way that was incredibly deep. She would often take walks in the backwoods of a small town in Vermont and talk with God for hours. My mother followed suit in her walk with God. She often encouraged me to pray for everything. Because of this upbringing, I seek God each day, listening to what He has to say. I can't imagine a day without God's leading and direction in my life. My passion for prayer, and ability to communicate the importance of prayer both personally and corporately is important, and now many are experiencing this powerful impact of prayer. I love **Proverbs 3:5-6** that says, ***"Trust in the Lord with all your heart, and lean not to your own understanding; In all your ways acknowledge Him, and He will direct your paths."*** The Lord has surely directed my paths, and in every path chosen, He has given me strength, knowledge, and encouragement.

My husband, Tim, and I have two Yorkies who are a part of our family and travel everywhere with us. I'm also a fan of football, NASCAR, and enjoy camping, hiking, kayaking, biking, and snowshoeing. I need that fresh air to keep me young — LOL!

CONTACT ME AT:
www.be-in-couraged.com
Email: jan@be-in-couraged.com
FaceBook: @praywithjan
Instagram: beincouraged411
YouTube: prayermomentswithjan
Tweet: #praywithjan

Be-IN-Couraged is an outreach of MSW Ministries, a 501(c)(3) organization

ACKNOWLEDGEMENTS

There are so many people I'd like to thank for being an integral part of my life personally, but the list would be lengthy, so please accept this huge THANK YOU to everyone in my life. However, there are a few individuals that I would be dishonoring if I didn't specifically thank. I have a huge heart of gratitude for each of these people:

Thank you, Bob and Gretchen Ravenscroft, for giving me the opportunity to indulge in my passion at Music Serving The Word Ministries. It is with great honor that I could be called your friend in Christ Jesus our Lord!

Thank you, Theresa Love, for encouraging me to write this book. Your support will always be appreciated.

Thank you, Maura Dean, for reminding me that my passion for encouraging others has always been guided by the Holy Spirit.

Thank you, Larissa Johnson, for assisting me with other projects so that I could actually get this book written.

Thank you, Tim Sherman, my beloved husband who is always by my side with encouragement and support. I could have never done this project without you.

Thank you, Pastor Bryan Bloom, for your guidance in my life over several heart-breaking years of my great loss.

Thank you, Jeremy Sherman and Kelly Fowler, for standing by me when I was figuring out our blended family and for loving me through that journey.

Thank you, my precious son, Brandon, for being the person God created you to be while you were on this earth. What an honor it was to be called your mother for nineteen years! Little did you know how much your love for life and God would continue to encourage so many people years after you met our Lord.

Lastly and most importantly, my life is filled with joy because of my Lord and Savior Jesus Christ who loves me unconditionally, who calls me wonderful, who says I am enough, and who has been with me all my life. I certainly would not be living today if I didn't have YOU!

INTRODUCTION

Dear Reader,

In the Kingdom of God, there is no loss. However, loss is a real thing. I know in my heart that the unwelcome loss in my life is somehow organized in the sight of the Lord, but in my eyes, I just see loss and a great deal of mess. Therefore, I call this unwelcome loss my organized mess. Everything that happens to us helps us gain understanding, wisdom, purpose, peace, strength, joy and so much more in Christ. The key is how we respond in our dealing with loss here on earth.

The best response that I've found to my unwelcome loss is a thankful heart filled with praise. **"The Lord gives, and the Lord takes away. Blessed be the name of the Lord" (Job 1:21).** All good things (possessions, family, friends, health, etc.) are gifts from God. We may sometimes feel that we are entitled to these possessions. Rather than sulking and complaining of what we've lost, maybe our response should be one of gratitude. I am reminded of God's relentless joy and most importantly to NEVER let go of His loving hand.

After all is said and done, I've come to realize that there can be joy in the midst of our loss. The seasons of loss in our lives can end up being the joy we've longed for. Over my years of loss, I have gained so much joy. Psalms 16:11 tells us that we can have the Lord's fullness of joy by spending time in His presence. That is the key . . . spend more time in the presence of the Lord. This brings joy and peace to an otherwise hectic and hurtful season of our organized mess. When I'm in need of joy, I can withdraw some of it from deep within my heart. This is what gets me through those days of difficulty.

My prayer for you is that you will also spend time in the presence of the Lord and seek His face. Start by thanking God for the things that give you joy and for the people in your life. Then tell Him your hurts and pain. Allow His love to give you comfort and peace. Sometimes just being quiet with God heals the soul. This is where you will find your joy. **"Draw near to God, and He will draw near to you"** is what **James 4:8** says. Take that to heart and spend time with God in prayer and just be in His presence. Trust that He knows what is best for his child. Take that leap of faith and trust in His name.

I wrote this book for you! I tell many short stories of the organized mess in my life in hopes it will give you a little encouragement to face the unwelcome loss that's staring you down. I truly believe that there is joy in the midst of our mess or loss, but it's how we respond that gets us through the tough times. I pray that you will also be reminded of God's great love and joy for you.

In His Magnificent Name,
Jan Sherman

TABLE OF CONTENTS

LIFE WITH BRANDON

The Joy Moments / The Long-Awaited
Birth of My Son 3

The Devastating Organized Mess of Divorce 5

Being a Single Parent. 9

I want to Be Like You 12

Veggies For Lunch? 14

God Knows His Child's Voice 16

Kisses From Heaven 18

I Got This. 20

I Love Him More 23

My Church Family 25

Joy After So Much Organized Mess 28

JAN SHERMAN

A Miscarriage?.......................... 30

Let Go and Let God 32

Does Your Kite Fly?...................... 34

Green Lights and Blue Skies 37

Do You See The Beauty? 39

It Stinks 41

LIFE WITHOUT BRANDON

The Great Organized Mess................ 47

Rest in God's Hands 52

The Lord is Near........................ 54

Have You Prayed About It? 56

In His Presence......................... 58

My Role Model.......................... 61

MORE UNWELCOME LOSS

Rejection 65

Loneliness.............................. 68

My Yorkshire Terrier 70

My Dad 72

My Inspiring Mom 75

Unexpected Life Journeys 78

LIFE NOW WITH ENCOURAGEMENT

Scars From Our Unwelcome Loss 83

A Heart of Gratitude. 85

Stay in His Presence 88

Laugh Often. 90

God is Good! 92

You Are Good Enough! 94

There is A Season 96

Hinds' Feet on High Places 98

A Life Worth Watching. 100

Choices. 102

Don't Worry 104

Find The Joy in Every Organized Mess. 107

LIFE WITH BRANDON

LIFE WITH BRANDON

THE JOY MOMENTS / THE LONG-AWAITED BIRTH OF MY SON

It was one week before the due date of my son's birth, and my water broke. The long-awaited nine months of carrying a child were soon going to end, and I anxiously looked forward to holding my baby in my arms. After twenty-three hours of intense pain and a few minor problems, my son was born. Laughter filled the hospital room when the first words out of my mouth were, "It's a baby!" The doctor said, "Well, of course it is, and he is a healthy baby at that!" The joy of my life had finally arrived, and I decided to call him Brandon Robert, meaning "from the beacon hill, bright and shining."

I wanted everyone to know that my son was born weighing 7lbs 11oz and was 20 inches long. He was perfect, and I wanted the world to know how excited I was for the beautiful gift I was given. Little did I know how much of "a beacon on a hill" he would be later in his life to so many people. I remember every little detail of that day, and the long hours of labor that I had to endure. It reminded me of the many scriptures that talk about those who labor. One of those scriptures I've always appreciated is found in Matthew 11:28 that states "Come to Me, all you who labor and are heavy laden, and I will give you rest." I understood just how much rest was needed after the intense labor I experienced in childbearing. I was exhausted, yet beautifully happy having my son in my arms once and for all.

We took Brandon home a couple of days after birth and began the process of figuring out how to be a parent to a tiny, helpless child who needed me 100% for his existence. It was a wonderful yet terrifying experience for me, a then 21-year-old woman. And so, the journey of motherhood began. This was the most joyful time of my life!

Think for a moment of a beautiful time in your life that gave you or continues to give you joy. Did you have to labor before your joy appeared? Spend some time thanking the Lord for your joy. These times of joy are what God gives as a reprieve and a portion of rest from the hardships of life.

MATTHEW 11:28

Come to Me, all you who labor and are heavy laden, and I will give you rest.

> **Be-IN-Couraged and enjoy those moments of joy and happiness that are given to you!**

LIFE WITH BRANDON
THE DEVASTATING ORGANIZED MESS OF DIVORCE

When Brandon turned two years old, there was something very wrong with my marriage. My husband was gone most of the time leaving me to care for our son alone. At first, I was okay doing that job alone because I loved being a mom. Brandon was changing all the time, and he had already started walking. It was a wonderful time for me.

As the months went by, I knew that my husband was becoming more and more distant. He began drinking and going out with his work friends who drank a lot. Our doctor warned my husband that if he didn't stop drinking, he would be six feet under the ground within a year. But this news didn't stop him. He drank more and got in trouble with the police many times.

I had to live and keep my focus on caring for my son. I was incredibly hurt and didn't know what to do next. My husband began controlling my every move. He didn't want me anymore, but he felt as though he had to control what I did and where I went. I was held captive in my own home, all the while trying to be the best mother I knew how to be at that point.

There were rumors at work; a place where we both held full-time jobs, and everyone knew us. The rumor was that my husband was having an affair. Then, the unthinkable happened. I found out that my husband was indeed unfaithful to me. Of course, it was everyone's responsibility to tell me. I wanted to scream, "Enough! No more noise!"

I was alone with the emptiness in my heart and the feeling of not being good enough overflowed my mind. I cried every night as I tried to figure out what went wrong, and what I did to allow this man to control me as he did. I spent time with God crying, screaming, and doing a lot of listening, which didn't come easy.

Eight months later, on New Year's Eve, my husband told me he no longer loved me and had decided to leave. He wanted a divorce. He went on to say that he had chosen not to be a husband or a father at this time in his life and that he just wanted to enjoy the single life again. Really? We just built a house and bought a new car. All of our expenses took two incomes, and now he's telling me he wants a divorce? He left that night, and I cried myself to sleep on the couch.

When I woke up, I felt the arms of Jesus wrapped around me, holding me like a baby. It was the most comforting feeling I had ever felt, and it was real. The Lord spoke to me in my mind, letting me know that even though I had lost my husband, God still loved me, and He would never leave me. I fell asleep again and somehow woke up in my bed that following morning. Divorce stinks, but even through the tough times of my divorce, I knew I had the Lord to lean on, and I had to learn to trust that He was always with me, which I doubted many times.

Was this the loss I had feared? Yes! The next year was devastating with regards to finding a lawyer, several court dates, and even my husband coming back in my home and abusing me both physically and verbally. He had become an alcoholic, and when he drank, he got violently angry. This anger was taken out on me physically, and I had all I could do to protect my son from seeing what was going on. At that time, I could hardly take care of myself, let alone my son who was then three.

Thoughts kept going through my mind of how I was the first in my family to get a divorce, and how I was never good enough. These thoughts were not coming from God, and God continued to show me His love and to care for Brandon and me. One thing I learned was that it was okay not to be ok. This was a long journey that I had to walk, but I wasn't alone. God reminded me often that He was with me — always, but I was badly wounded, and I had to be reminded of this message over and over again.

Over the next few years, I became severely depressed and was anorexic and bulimic. I had lost a lot of weight, and one day I was looking for my belt but couldn't find it. I went into my six-year-old son's closet and tried on his belt. It fit! Somehow, in my way of thinking, this was good, but clearly, it wasn't. This was the beginning of my unhealthy weight loss.

I was certain that God was gone. I didn't feel Him, and if He really loved me the way I was taught growing up in the church, then He wouldn't allow such devastating events to happen to me, right? As I look back on this very difficult time in my life, I realize that God was indeed with me, and closer to me than I knew. His hand of protection was evident, and He showed me His great love and taught me how to be a single mom. This took time, but the inner fight of not being good enough wasn't over, it had just begun.

Can you relate to this kind of loss in your life? How has your life been changed by your devastating loss? Can you see how God has been with you through these turbulent times? I assure you that you've never been alone. God cares for you more than you know, and He only wants you to accept His love in your life. Look to God and ask Him to reveal His love to you today.

LAMENTATIONS 3:32

Though he brings grief, he also shows compassion because of the greatness of his unfailing love.

HEBREWS 13:5

I will never leave you nor forsake you.

> **Be-IN-Couraged and know that God is with you all the time!**

LIFE WITH BRANDON
BEING A SINGLE PARENT

Being a single parent isn't easy. In fact, it's downright difficult! I was adjusting to a recent divorce, and I had no clue what I was doing. I didn't know how I was going to get Brandon to daycare and me to work, all before 8:00 a.m. without any help. But I managed. God helped me plan out a routine, and I had to stick with it.

This awkward and incredibly lonely season in my life lasted five years. Five years of being a single parent and not having a clue how or what to do next. I just did what I had to do without thinking too much. I realized I had the most important job ever and no one else was going to do it if I didn't. It was a job of being a mom to a young child who needed me to know when to go to bed, when to wake up, and when to eat. I had to figure out when to say yes and when to say no. The list goes on and on, and the incapability of doing this job full-time became my reality. Discouragement and exhaustion set in, but I kept pushing through because I knew Brandon needed me.

As difficult as it was being a single parent, there were little moments of joy that crept up, and I found myself laughing with Brandon. God gave me something to look forward to every day, and I did the best I knew how under the circumstances. One thing I had on my side is that Brandon didn't know any different. How I brought up Brandon was okay to him. I was so grateful that my mom was just a phone call away to help guide me through the process of parenthood. And that she did! She was my mother, full of love and wisdom, and she shared all of it with me.

I carved out time to play and "pretend" with my son. He loved his trains, and it was great to see him use his imagination with me. I was so proud of who he was — my son! I loved being a mom and would ask God to help me in this vital role every day. It was important to me to show Brandon unconditional love so he could grow up to love others in that same way. We prayed together, played together, laughed and cried together. I was finally seeing the joy of being Brandon's mom come back to life. It was wonderful.

Whether we played with trains, built forts outside, or just watched a kid-friendly movie together, I put him first. He was my pride and joy, and I wanted to make sure he knew it. Yes, there were planned bedtimes, but there were days when I surprised him and let him stay up an extra hour. Most of those times, he fell asleep in my arms, but it was wonderful to give my young child a little-unexpected joy.

As desperate as I was to love my child the absolute best way I could, God also showed me how much He loved me. God desired then just as He desires now that my attention be always focused on Him. He will bring the joy into my life just when I need it. Sometimes, He brings me joy when I'm not expecting it, and I'm always on the lookout for these special moments of joy.

ORGANIZED MESS

PROVERBS 22:6

Train up a child in the way he should go, and when he is old, he will not depart from it.

> Be-IN-Couraged! Train your children in the way God leads you. Look for the times that bring you laughter and rest in those moments of pure joy!

LIFE WITH BRANDON
I WANT TO BE LIKE YOU

Mmm, I can smell those fresh-baked cookies now. When I think of cookies coming out of the oven, my mind goes to when Brandon was eight. He loved to be in the kitchen with me and bake cookies and brownies with my assistance. He was so happy to stir the ingredients and try the inevitable job of cracking an egg without getting the shell pieces in the mixture. It was one of our mom-son times that we had together, and I treasure those times in my heart. Brandon was young and wanted to learn from his mom, which gave me a cheerful heart that sang for joy!

One day while we were making chocolate chip cookies, Brandon looked up at me and said, "Momma, when I grow up, I want to be a cooker just like you." With that said, I did my best not to laugh out loud. A cooker? How funny! I loved to cook and bake, and so did my son. My heart burst with joy because he wanted to be just like me.

That got me thinking of how our Heavenly Father must smile when we express how we want to be more like Jesus. I wonder if He laughs with me when I say things like that. I wonder how much He admires His children when all they want is to be more like Him. I don't think I could ever comprehend how much He loves me, but that day when my son told me that he wanted to be just like me when he grew up made me a proud parent.

ORGANIZED MESS

I see how a cheerful heart can be good medicine. A good laugh is better than a complaining voice. Lord, help me to laugh more and seek a heart more like yours.

PROVERBS 17:22
A cheerful heart is good medicine.

> **Be-IN-Couraged and seek the Lord your God with all your heart. I pray that as you spend time with God that you desire to be more like Him!**

LIFE WITH BRANDON
VEGGIES FOR LUNCH?

From the moment Brandon was born, I wanted to be that perfect mom. In fact, if Brandon would have a temper tantrum in front of my friends, I'd be so embarrassed that I'd want to crawl under the table. How could a mother let her son scream in front of others? What am I doing wrong? I was determined to be the best mom possible, and at those moments I felt as though I was letting my son down. Why? I didn't need to prove to anyone that I was a good mom. I knew I was. At least I was the best mom I could be. The task of bringing up my son as a single parent was not easy.

In order to survive, I had to let go of a lot of parental things like veggies for lunch. That's right; I only gave my son vegetables for dinner. Don't judge me. Brandon became a very well-rounded person as though I knew what I was doing all along. Truth be known, I didn't know what I was doing at all. I had all I could do to function for myself, let alone bring up a child. But God had other ideas. He brought people into my life to help me, and to give assistance when I needed it most.

It was ok for me to say I can't do this alone. I'm no super mom, and I'm proud of that. I'm who I am, and I did the best I knew how to bring up my son in a good way, but I was not perfect. Yes, Brandon stayed up late at times as we made brownies and put a scoop of ice cream on top. Yes, he had a few temper tantrums. No, I didn't always give him veggies — certainly not for lunch. However, we took road trips, played board games, took walks, and plainly put, we had fun. I made my son a priority, and that's what made the difference in his life. I would do anything for him. I didn't want him to be sad or lonely or unloved. I loved him with great love and took care of him to the best of my ability.

If you're struggling to be that perfect person to someone, I encourage you to run far away from that idea. You'll never be perfect. No one will be, as long as we are on this planet called Earth. Be who you were created to be. Ask for help when needed, and most of all, love others with an indescribable love. Don't worry about eating veggies for lunch, although I do now!

PHILIPPIANS 4:13

I can do all things through Christ who strengthens me.

> **Be-IN-Couraged and be the person God created you to be, and don't worry if things aren't perfect!**

LIFE WITH BRANDON
GOD KNOWS HIS CHILD'S VOICE

As Brandon grew up, we would often joke around trying to imitate accents of actors and dialects from around the world. At the most awkward times, Brandon would whip out an accent from Australia or Ireland and make us all belly laugh. I was always amazed at how good he got imitating different dialects and voices. Talent? Not so sure about that, but we had fun and laughed a lot in the process! With all the voices Brandon did, there was one voice that I knew more than any other. It was his original voice. As a mom, there was no mistaking my son's voice!

God knows His children's voices too. When we are in an urgent situation, and we cry out to God, He hears us! When we are happy, He hears our laughter! Not only does He hear our voice, but He responds and lets us know He is there. How comforting is that? Brandon was always comforted when he knew I heard his voice. Whether he was in a panic or just laughing, I recognized his voice and responded to him.

In Numbers 20:16 the children of Israel said, "When we cried out to the Lord, He heard our voice and sent the Angel and brought us up out of Egypt." God is always with us! This brings me so much comfort knowing that God is with me through the tough times, as well as the times of laughter.

Trust in the fact that God hears your voice and will respond to your need. He loves to hear our voices, so let's purposefully spend more time talking with Him and enjoy being in His presence.

HEBREWS 13:5
I will never leave you nor forsake you.

> **Be-IN-Couraged! Know that God is with you. Laugh often and thank God for the funny things in life!**

LIFE WITH BRANDON
KISSES FROM HEAVEN

Our children ask a lot of questions. Teaching Brandon about life the way he was able to comprehend it was sometimes a challenge. When Brandon was young, he asked questions . . . a lot of questions. Sometimes I wouldn't know the answer, or maybe just didn't take the time to explain a detailed answer to him so I would just say **"BECAUSE."** Ever been there? However, Brandon was a very persistent child, and so his response to my "Because" answer was always **"WHY CAUSE?"**

One time when he was very young, he asked me to explain rain. Ok, so how do you explain rain to a three-year-old? I knew that the whole chemical and physical properties of clouds would be too much for him to comprehend, so I kept it simple, and my response was "Raindrops are kisses from Heaven."

Since that time, when it rains, I say God is kissing me on the head, or arm. Yes, I still say that to this day. In fact, it was raining this morning, and that's what I thought. God gave me kisses from Heaven because He cares that much for me even on a day I'm not particularly or deliberately talking to Him. It's become my treasured saying every time it rains. It always follows with a smile on my face thinking about Brandon and how he accepted kisses from Heaven as the explanation of rain.

Just like a child, our questions may be simple or profound and reflect our curious nature about the mysteries and wonders of our universe — God's creation. God never asked us to wander blindly through life and never discourages the questions we have of things that are puzzling to us. However, when you are three years old and asking about rain, a dissertation on cumulus clouds with the chemical and physical properties of precipitation and atmospheric condensation will most assuredly be met with a thousand more questions. Like a good parent, God will only reveal what He knows we can comprehend.

Even for the difficult issues we face, a simple answer such as, "raindrops are kisses from heaven," may be the response He knows will give us a moment of joy and strength to endure the storm. Simple joys and simple pleasures are wrapped up in God's care for us. He only gives us what we can handle, and in most cases, His answers bring us relief from our incessant curiosity about things we just cannot understand — perhaps even courage to face the things we fear.

God brings His children joy in many ways . . . kisses from heaven is just one-way for me. Psalm 21:1 talks about the strength and joy we have in the Lord. My days can be chaotic and difficult, but in the middle of all the chaos, I can find joy in the Lord. Why not ask God for a special joy for you? Ask for His joy that will give you something to smile about in the middle of your chaotic day. Wishing you kisses from heaven today, whether it's raining or not.

PSALM 16:11

In Your presence, there is fullness of joy.

Be-IN-Couraged in the fact that God is faithfully answering your questions knowing that the answers will become clearer as you grow in Him.

LIFE WITH BRANDON
I GOT THIS

Baby showers are great. It's a way for your family and friends to gift you with items needed for your new baby. At my baby shower, a friend gave me a stuffed animal for my baby boy. It was a dog named Daffney. After the first several months, Brandon would hug Daffney and rub the silk tag up close to his ear and fall asleep. Brandon loved Daffney and took her everywhere he went.

When Brandon was two or three, he came to me with tears in his eyes. He held Daffney in one hand and the silk tag in the other. He was devastated, and it broke my heart. All I could think of was "I got this." I knew how to sew and mend things . . . no biggie! But how could I convince my upset son that everything was going to be all right? After many tears and hugs, I told Brandon that Daffney would need some surgery and that I could help mend her brokenness. Brandon's sadness started to change, and he was later overcome with gladness when I brought little Daffney back to him all mended.

The Lord also tells us "I got this" when we come to Him in prayer with our brokenness. It's no biggie to Him, but it's our job to hand our hurts and brokenness over to Him so He can do His surgery in our lives. This is not easy, but if we allow God to do His work of healing and mending, we will be overcome with gladness once again. How do we do this? How do we start the process of giving God our unwelcome loss, hurts, and brokenness? It begins with the knowledge that God wants us to be free from our bondage of loss. It begins knowing that we're not alone and that God is with us. Sometimes it takes me quoting scripture or saying the name of Jesus over and over or listening to great music that encourages me. Sometimes the process of healing begins when I'm talking with a safe person who cares for me, whether it's a family member or close friend. Whatever it is for you, do it until you sense that God does care and that He is there to take our hurts and disappointments. He will surely replace all of our loss with the power of His healing hands.

I still have Daffney to this day and am reminded how much God cares about the little things in our lives and how much He wants us to go to Him when we are broken. Just as I could easily mend Daffney's tag, God is easily able to mend our brokenness as long as we go to Him and ask Him. He is closer to us than we realize and desires to show His power in our lives. Why are we willing to have everyone else try and "fix" our problems, but don't go to God until we are at our wits-end? Why is it that we sometimes have that tendency to go to God last, when all He wants is for us to go to Him first? Why are we so willing to waste time trying to fix things ourselves then later find out that we cannot completely heal our brokenness?

Are you in need of some mending today? Why not talk to God and tell Him what hurts? If you are crushed, He will be there and give you the peace and comfort needed this day.

PSALM 34:28

The Lord is near to those who have a broken heart and saves those who are crushed in spirit.

> Be-IN-Couraged and know that God says "I GOT THIS" and He is in control!

LIFE WITH BRANDON
I LOVE HIM MORE

It was summer, and I had to make one of the most difficult decisions of my life. I had to put my six-year-old son on a plane to fly three thousand miles to see his biological father. I struggled for weeks with this decision. How could I put my baby on a plane all alone? I knew the airlines were set up to take care of children, but this was a very long flight with a plane change in the middle of the country. Brandon was my baby, and I always wanted to be with him. This was different. I couldn't be with him. I had to let him go alone. Would he be ok? Would he cry and miss his momma? These questions haunted me for weeks, but the time came when I had to pack his bags and begin the process of preparing for an enormously difficult transition. Brandon seemed ok with going on a plane alone, but I sure wasn't.

I was at church the week before Brandon's flight and remember crying out to God to protect my baby! I remember the conversation I had with God. It was in my mind that I felt Him ask me, "Jan, how much do you love your son?" Ok, so I thought this was a stupid question. I'm his mother. I love him to the ends of the world and back! No one could love him more! Then I heard God say, "I do. I love him more."

I immediately stopped crying and gasped trying to get air into my lungs to breathe. God clearly made His point, and at that moment, I felt a peace that could only come from God. God loves my son more than I could ever love him. It was a mind-blowing reassurance and a reality check that I needed in order to put my Brandon on that plane and be away from him for two months. My job was to trust in God and what He told me. I could not worry or be anxious, although I have to admit that it was extraordinarily difficult for me.

God did take care of my son, and He showed me that He did love him more than I ever could! God also loves me more than anyone ever could on this planet. This gives me great peace and the ability to trust in Him more each day. Do you need some reassurance that God loves you and those close to you more than anyone else ever could? Step out and trust Him today. He won't fail you!

PHILIPPIANS 4:7

And the peace of God, which transcends all understanding, will guard your hearts and your minds in Christ Jesus.

ROMANS 8:38-39

I am persuaded that neither death nor life, nor angels nor principalities nor powers, nor things present nor things to come, nor height nor depth, nor any other created thing shall be able to separate us from the love of God, which is in Christ Jesus our Lord.

> **Be-IN-Couraged today and trust that God loves you and those you love more than you'll ever know.**

LIFE WITH BRANDON
MY CHURCH FAMILY

Prayer has always been a top priority in my family. My grandmother passed away when my mother was seventeen years old, and therefore I had never met her. However, I'd hear countless stories of how my grandmother would go into the backwoods of her old Vermont home to pray. This was where she met with God in a very personal way. Mom would tell me that they would never worry how long she was gone, or even where she was, because when she arrived back home, the presence of the Lord was evident in her countenance. She experienced God on a regular basis! My mother took on the mantle of prayer from my grandmother, and prayer was what she practiced daily!

After my divorce, I was distraught and discouraged, so I contacted the pastor at my church to pray with me and to help me. Soon after asking, they appeared on my doorstep. However, when I told them that I went to my family doctor who prescribed anti-depressants, they refused to support me. In fact, they gave me the ultimatum of either stop seeing my doctor, or I couldn't be a part of the church any longer. This was a shock to me and certainly didn't help with my recovery. My sisters and parents lived in different states, which added to my loneliness. I was unmistakably a wreck and alone.

My doctor called my mother who lived several states away and told her to come and stay with me. My doctor was afraid that I would take my life and knew that I was close to my mom. Mom packed up her bags and drove to my home the very next day. She stayed with me for six weeks. I don't remember much about those six weeks except that she would talk to my dad every day and gave him updates on how I was doing. Mom took care of Brandon when I couldn't and kept up the house — cleaning, laundry, etc.

What happened next was none short of a miracle. Mom prayed, and God intervened. He had other plans for my life, and it included joy. This is the part of my story that gets exciting — the prayer part and the pure joy that followed afterward.

Mom got a call from my dad saying how he'd received a letter from our long-term friends in Arizona. That family and our family were as close as a peanut butter and jelly sandwich. This close family moved to Arizona in 1974, and my heart was crushed. Why? Because when I was ten years old, my first boyfriend was the son of this family. His name was Tim. Every year after they moved to Arizona, my Mom would send a Christmas letter to them. During the timeframe that Mom stayed with me, she wrote another Christmas letter and penned in a personal note on the bottom asking them to pray for me. Tim saw the letter, picked it up, and after reading it, he immediately felt that he had to write to my parents and see if it would be all right for him to get in contact with me again. Now, this had been years since they moved, and Tim got married and recently divorced just like me. He had been through some really tough times and thought he'd share his stories with me. Mom asked me if I would be ok receiving a letter from Tim, and I remember very clearly thinking, "Okay, but nothing is going to help me at this point."

Now my Mom also kept a prayer journal and wrote dates next to her prayers. A few days after my parents told Tim it would be ok for him to contact me my Mom felt a strong urge to pray on the inside and outside of my home. She wrote this down in her prayer journal and asked God for an answer that day! Bold? Yes, but God heard her bold prayer and answered it. Years later my Mom took out that prayer journal, and I found the first letter from Tim. They were both dated the same day! God answered her prayers and sent me a man who truly loved me!

Yes, I had a loss in the church family, but God sent me my biological family to aid in bringing joy into my life once again. That was the beginning of my prayer life. I knew that Mom was relentless in praying, and I wanted to be the same way.

Are you in a situation where you feel stuck like there's no hope in sight? I have great news for you! God is there to meet your need. He will make a way when there seems to be no way. How that happens is a mystery to me, but I pray that you will wait for the answer and know that God is there to provide for you just like He did for me that day so many years ago.

GALATIANS 6:2

Bear one another's burdens, and so fulfill the law of Christ.

Be-IN-Couraged and don't be embarrassed to ask for prayer. Others are willing to be there and pray for you even if you can't pray for yourself.

LIFE WITH BRANDON
JOY AFTER SO MUCH ORGANIZED MESS

After eighteen months of writing letters and dating, Tim and I got married. It was a wonderfully exciting day. I was marrying my childhood sweetheart and loved his family that I had known for years. The wedding day was like a family reunion between my family and Tim's family. My son, Brandon and Tim's two children, Jeremy and Kelly got along well, and they were all a part of this very special day. Blended families are not easy, but with God in the middle of our marriage, we worked through those difficult times. How? Tim and I both purposefully put God first no matter what, and we always go to Him in prayer before any decisions are made in our marriage. This didn't happen right away, but over time we understood how important that choice was. It strengthened our marriage and caused us to examine ourselves as a married couple on a regular basis.

The first few months we were so happy . . . we were honeymooners and life couldn't get any better, right? We took trips with the kids, went to the beach that was four blocks from our home, and created memories we all smile (or laugh) about even now. God gave us time away from all of our losses to enjoy life a little. He brought joy into our lives that had been absent for so long. He continued to show us how much He loved us and we responded by spending more time with God. After all, relationships are a two-way street. My first marriage fell apart because God was pulled from being the center, and therefore it was pretty near impossible to keep the purity and love that God desired in that marriage. This time around was going to be different, and I wanted to tell everyone about this amazing event in my life!

Tim and I started by sharing how stubborn we both were, and recognized that if this was going to work, we had to be honest and kept communicating on every issue in our lives. Communication is vital in any relationship, whether it's a sister, mother, spouse, friend or God. We agreed that this would take determination and practice and we were willing to do our best to talk, read scripture and pray together.

We continue our open communication to this day. We've found things to do together. We love going to the movie theatre, kayaking, hiking, riding our bikes, snowshoeing, and camping. We enjoy each other's company after more than 26 years and encourage each other when needed. We're not perfect, but have worked hard in making our marriage one that is filled with happiness! Joy — yes! Pure joy!

I CHRONICLES 16:24

Publish his glorious deeds among the nations. Tell everyone about the amazing things he does.

Be-IN-Couraged! Be thankful and create a heart of gratitude for the times that are great!

LIFE WITH BRANDON
A MISCARRIAGE?

I was thirty-one when Tim and I married, and Brandon was eight years old. Things were great until I got pregnant. Don't get me wrong. I wanted another baby, but that would mean that there would be nine years difference between my two birth children and thirteen years difference between our oldest son and our new baby. Starting over again with another baby was a difficult thought to process. However, we accepted this new life and began to plan for her delivery.

Thirteen weeks later I miscarried. This was devastating. We just got used to the fact that a baby would be a part of our family, and she was gone. My employment at that time wasn't helpful and wouldn't give me sick leave to grieve. What was I supposed to do? It was a very long time before I felt normal again. After all, I just lost a person who was a part of my flesh and blood.

I prayed and prayed and asked God to help me with this loss. I had no idea how to deal with it. It was as if someone dropped into my hands this intense grief and expected me to figure out how to move forward on my own. Our child was gone, and we had to go on with our lives. At least that's the message I heard over and over again . . . Life goes on. This was a mystery to me. I thought, "how does life go on when life was just lost?" Maybe everyone else's life goes on, but not mine. I was stuck in the loss of my child, but that old saying "time heals" is true. Time did heal our brokenness, but the memory of our unborn child still exists today.

ORGANIZED MESS

God, once again, came to my rescue. He gave me the strength to endure each new day and showed me how to find joy in my loss. Tim and I grew stronger together. I'm not saying it was easy because it wasn't! Some days were more difficult than others, and we had to fight our way through those days just to stay above water.

Psalm 30:5 was given to me, and it says ***"Weeping may endure for a night, but joy comes in the morning."*** I remember feeling peace from God. My circumstances did not change, but my perspective had. God met me where I was and gave me peace that passed all my understanding and eventually a joy grew inside of me that also didn't make sense. This is how I know it was God. I felt immense supernatural love, and I knew I would be ok.

PSALM 30:5

Weeping may endure for a night, but joy comes in the morning.

> **Be-IN-Couraged and remember that true, pure joy is not dependent on your circumstances!**

LIFE WITH BRANDON
LET GO AND LET GOD

Blended families are not easy. In fact, they are downright difficult! I was a single mom with one son, Brandon, and my newly married husband had two children from a previous marriage. At first, I thought, "This is great! Brandon will have a sister and a brother to play with, and he will finally get a Dad that loves him and will spend time with him." But this wasn't exactly the case. These relationships didn't come naturally, and they took a very long time to grow into the family I always wanted. In fact, the relationship between Brandon and Tim wasn't what I had hoped for at all.

I did everything in my power to bring my new husband and son together so we could be one happy family, but nothing was working. I became exhausted, and at one point, I just wanted to throw my arms up in defeat! Three years went by, and I found myself talking to God. I said, "I can't do this any longer. I have to give this relationship to you." I begged God to perform a miracle between these two people that I loved the most. I realized that I had to give it to God and for Him to take it and heal all the broken hearts involved. This was exactly what God wanted me to do. He had been so patient, and I had been so miserable trying to do it myself. Finally, I caved and washed my hands of trying to make something happen. That's when God gave me peace. He didn't give me a quick answer, just peace.

ORGANIZED MESS

About a year later we were in church, and the pastor whispered in my husband's ear to go and pray with Brandon. My husband refused at first, but when the pastor came a second time to encourage him to pray with Brandon, he finally gave in. Truthfully, I'm not sure he wanted to walk up in front of the church to kneel and pray with Brandon, but he did it. At that moment I knew God stepped in and performed a miracle. Rivers of tears began to flow from both Brandon and Tim, and the healing process began.

You see, I had to give their relationship to God, and my husband had to give in to God for our miracle to take place. It wasn't my timing, but it was God's perfect timing. From that point on, their relationship was closer than ever, and God was smack dab in the middle of it. Do you believe in miracles? I do, and my family is living proof of a miracle in action. Yes, blended families are difficult, but if you give it to God and let go, He will do the impossible! Don't stop praying!

I PETER 5:7

Casting all your care on Him, for He cares for you.

ROMANS 12:12

Let your hope make you glad. Be patient in time of trouble and never stop praying.

> **Be-IN-Couraged! Let go of whatever you're trying to make happen. Let God do it in His way and in His time**

LIFE WITH BRANDON
DOES YOUR KITE FLY?

One day our three kids wanted to go to the store and buy something they could play with. Tim and I decided to give them a dollar amount to spend, and it was up to each one to figure out what they wanted to buy. Our daughter bought a paint set and some beach toys. The two boys decided that they wanted a kite to fly at the beach. Each child purchased their item, and then we went home.

That afternoon our daughter started painting, and Tim helped the boys put their kites together. By the time they were carefully assembled and ready to fly, it was getting late in the day, so we decided to wait until the next day to go to the beach.

After breakfast the following morning, we all set out towards the beach. Our daughter brought her newly purchased beach shovels, buckets, and sand rakes and immediately began to build her sand castle. The day was not as breezy as the day before, but Tim still thought there would be enough wind to fly the boys' kites. After a few tries, Brandon gave up, put his kite down and played in the sand. However, our oldest boy was persistent. All he could think about was how high his kite would fly. He was determined and ran with the kite over and over again only to realize that there was no wind to carry it any distance. He fell to his knees in discouragement as Tim consoled him.

It was at this time that Brandon said something none of us will forget. He said, "You know, sometimes your kite just doesn't wanna go up." This was profound for an eight-year-old, but I didn't realize how profound at that time. That statement has been said over and over again by all of us in our family — even today I find myself saying, "You know, sometimes your kite just doesn't wanna go up."

In our individual lives, we want so desperately to have our kites fly high all the time and have everything turn out perfect. But perfection is not reality. Nothing is perfect, and everyone encounters a problem at least once in his or her life. Sometimes our kites won't go up at all, but that's ok. When we fall, we just need to get back up and try again. When there's no wind, maybe we need to pause and wait on the Lord to give us the element of wind needed to fly our kites. Eventually, they will fly, and we experience love, laughter, joy, and peace.

Does your kite fly today? If not, don't be discouraged. It will soon fly, and you will have contentment again. Keep your focus on God and allow Him to decide when your kite will fly and when it's time to wait.

The frustration in our oldest son subsided that day, and he was ok. Our boys eventually saw their kites fly, and we, as parents, were excited in their joy. I learned a big lesson that day on the beach; a lesson of patience and timing for the wind that we could not predict. When God asks us to wait, I pray that we will be obedient and wait for His wind to fly our kites again. Oh, the joy of that day!

JOHN 16:22

So, with you: Now is your time of grief, but I will see you again, and you will rejoice, and no one will take away your joy.

Be-IN-Couraged! Your kite will indeed fly again.

LIFE WITH BRANDON
GREEN LIGHTS AND BLUE SKIES

As a single mom, I did my best to guide my son and encourage him to make great decisions in his life. Because of this, Brandon grew up having a positive way of looking at things. Somehow, he would find the good in everyone, and the good in every situation.

As often as we could, we would both sit at the edge of his bed and flop back looking up at the ceiling. This was where we'd have our talks. This was where we'd laugh and cry. This was where we'd pray together. Brandon would ask me questions, and we'd discuss the upcoming life scenarios of friends and jobs. He wanted my opinion, and as his mother, I wanted to share as much as I could about life and advise him on certain situations.

I remember one time in particular how he wanted to show me a video that he did with his friends. At one point in the video, I noticed how a girl responded to something he had said. Probably a comment he should have avoided. As we talked about it, he very kindly excused himself and headed to his room. I thought I made him upset or angry because I brought this to his attention. However, what I found out a few minutes later made my heart burst with joy. Brandon excused himself to make a phone call to this girl and apologized to her. He saw his wrong choice of words that were used and didn't waste any time to make it right. You know how that made me feel? It made me feel like, wow, my son listens to me and wants to do what is right. Isn't this what every parent wants?

Brandon would try his best to be a positive person. He used to say, "Green lights and blue skies." This meant that whatever life throws your way, look at the positive. Whatever unwelcome loss comes your way, put a smile on your face and hold on to your companion called JOY. This is what Brandon did during his teen years, and this is what I hope to do every day of my life.

Green lights and blue skies have stuck with me over the years, and even now I will frequently say "Today is an all green lights and blue skies kind of a day." It puts a smile on my face and reminds me to see the positive in every situation. There is a positive in every situation. There are green lights and blue skies if you look deep enough. Can you find your green lights and blue skies today? Take a few minutes to ponder this statement, and if necessary, ask God to show you the positive in what you may be dealing with today.

PROVERBS 20:7

The godly walk with integrity; blessed are their children who follow them.

Be-IN-Couraged and look beyond the negative to see your green lights and blue skies in your day today!

LIFE WITH BRANDON
DO YOU SEE THE BEAUTY?

I'm sure you've heard that saying, "Beauty is in the eye of the beholder." Or what about, "One man's trash is another man's treasure?" These sayings got me thinking of a story when my husband and I took our three children to California on vacation many years ago. We took our motorhome and headed west. Our vacation that year was wonderful until the trip back home.

It was July and very hot, and the air conditioning in our motorhome was not working. This was our unwelcome loss that we did not expect. We had to find another way to keep cool, so the kids got spray bottles and filled them with cold water. They sprayed all of us with a fine mist for hours until we got home. We all had fun except for my husband. He didn't see the humor in losing our air conditioning and became rather grumpy. His joy from our vacation turned to disappointment and stress. He wasn't enjoying the heat and started complaining about the desert scenery we were driving through. His oldest son said something I'll never forget. He said, "Dad, the desert is beautiful. You just have to see the beauty!" From that point on we all tried to look at the beauty God made in the desert mountains. The kids even drew pictures of the mountains to remind us of our great vacation.

Remember that beauty is in the eye of the beholder! Is there a desert in your life that you have a difficult time seeing any beauty? It all comes down to what the eye of the beholder sees, and I pray that we'd all slow down and find the beauty in our desert through the eyes of the Lord. See what He has made in you. See what beautiful landscape He has created around you. See the beauty in others. How do we do that when we're in the middle of our desert? One way is to keep close to God. He promises to be near to us.

JAMES 4:8

Draw near to God, and He will draw near to you.

Be-IN-Couraged and take the time to draw close to God and see His beauty in everything!

LIFE WITH BRANDON
IT STINKS

If you've had children, you know that their favorite stuffed animal or blanket begins to look grimy and dirty, and at some point, you have to do something about that. Sometimes it has to be done creatively for you to take the item away from your child and clean it. I've thought that maybe when Brandon is sleeping or at school, I could get the chance to wash it.

As my son grew up, this cleaning process went from his beloved stuffed animal to his bedroom. I remember one time when I stepped into Brandon's room to find something; I almost gagged because it stunk so badly! I found food and dirty clothes under the bed and on the closet floor. I thought how is it so difficult to put dirty clothes in the basket for washing? Or why can't he at least put the dirty dishes in the kitchen sink and toss the uneaten food in the trash? Brandon's room needed a great deal of attention to get it clean again, and I was going to make sure he knew about it.

Brandon was embarrassed when I told him to clean up his room and air it out! He needed to do laundry and the dishes and clean up his act, and he knew it. After hearing the vacuum, smelling the air freshener, and noticing the dishes cleaned and put away, Brandon called me into his room. It was immaculate, and he was so proud to show me how he cleaned it up. I threw my arms around Brandon and told him how proud I was of him and how great of a job he did. He wanted my approval, and he got it.

This got me thinking about my spiritual life. Does it stink? Does it need a great deal of attention to get it cleaned up? Have I neglected areas of my life that aren't pleasing to the Lord? There has to come a time where I say, "Enough is enough — it stinks!" I have to come to my senses and desire to spend time with the Lord. Then maybe my life wouldn't stink so badly!

Luke chapter 15 tells a story of a man having two sons. The younger son received his portion of goods from his father and then left to do his own thing. He ended up in the fields feeding pigs, and from the lack of food, he even ate with the pigs. He stunk . . . literally, I'm sure. But when he came to his senses, he realized that he needed to be in the presence of his father. He returned home not knowing if his father would even accept him back. He thought that he'd most assuredly work as a servant, and he would be ok with that. At least he'd be fed and have a roof over his head. However, when he returned home, his father saw him from afar, ran to him and hugged and kissed him. He was given the best robe his father had. A ring was placed on his hand and shoes on his feet. His father wanted to make sure that this son knew he was loved and deeply missed!

I can imagine that this son only wanted to spend more time with his father after the welcoming home party that he received. This story encourages me to spend time with my Heavenly Father and listen to what He has to say. If He sees something in my life that stinks, I better pay attention!

What about you? Is there something in your life that stinks and needs some attention to clean it up? I encourage you to spend time with God and allow Him to speak into your life. Then accept what He has to say knowing that He is throwing His arms around you with love and desires for you to just be in His presence. He's got a robe, a ring, and new shoes waiting for you. Don't delay in doing what is right and see what God has in store for you this day.

LUKE 15:20

So he got up and went to his father. But while he was still a long way off, his father saw him and was filled with compassion for him; he ran to his son, threw his arms around him and kissed him.

> **Be-IN-Couraged! Spend time with the Lord and be washed in His great love for you!**

LIFE WITHOUT BRANDON

LIFE WITHOUT BRANDON
THE GREAT ORGANIZED MESS

I took the week before Memorial Day off from work to move into our new home in 2003. Brandon was done with college for the semester, so he was able to help us move. Even though he had to work in the afternoons, we had the mornings to spend together unpacking, talking and laughing together. When Brandon unpacked a box in his new room, he called me in to say, "Mom, come here and check this out." He wanted my opinion of where to hang his sports flags, Dale Earnhardt memorabilia and suggestions of what he would put behind his door and on his bulletin boards. He was excited to organize his closet. He measured out exactly where his new couch would go once we purchased it. It was good to be needed as Brandon's Mom. He was usually so busy with college, work, and friends that this week was our week, and I was determined to absorb every part of him in every way, especially when he called my name.

It was Sunday, May 25, 2003. I sang on the worship team at church and was tired by the end of the third service. When I got home from church, Brandon had already gone to work. I thought about how next week he'd have Sunday off, and that would be nice. Brandon called me on his way home from work to see what he would need to pick up at the grocery store to make tacos for the pool he lifeguarded at the next day — Memorial Day. Brandon got home with the food needed, and we both chopped the veggies and browned the meat for his Memorial Day party at work. As I stood in the hallway entrance, Brandon gave me a hug and kiss then walked out the door to leave and join the young adults from church for volleyball later that evening. He closed the door and then opened it back up. As Brandon looked at me, he said, "No, that's not good enough." He came back inside the house to give me another huge hug and kiss and told me that he loved me. That was so special! I thought, "I have such an awesome son!"

The way he came back in the door to hug me and tell me that he loved me will always resonate in my heart. Tim and I fell asleep early that night with exhaustion from moving, and before we knew it, morning took us by surprise and changed our lives forever.

It was 5:10 a.m. on Memorial Day May 26th when Tim and I awoke by the doorbell and someone knocking at our front door. I quickly got up, and Tim slowly began to get out of bed. As I walked down the hallway past Brandon's bedroom door, I saw that Brandon was not in his bed. My first thought was I must have locked the front door and Brandon didn't have his key. I opened up the door and my Yorkie, Dale ran out. As I called Dale back inside and picked him up, I saw the man who was knocking on our door. He proceeded to ask me if this was where Brandon lived. I said yes thinking Brandon got in trouble. Then he asked if I was his mother. My heart sunk as he continued to say that there had been an accident with a drunk driver and Brandon did not survive. I started to scream, and so did Tim who was right behind me. "NO, NO," I said over and over. I asked the detective if he was absolutely sure, and he gave me Brandon's backpack and wallet. I completely lost it and nearly fell to the

ORGANIZED MESS

floor. How could this have happened to my son — to Brandon? Oh God, no, this can't be true. Wake me up, Tim, please, no!

The detective was with us for quite some time, and as soon as he left, Tim and I got our phones and started calling our family. With tears rolling down our cheeks, our voices broke up trying to tell them that our Brandon had been killed by a drunk driver at 1:37 that morning. The news of losing our nineteen-year-old son was so painful! We had our other children and family over to be with us, but the unforeseen event of Brandon's life that came to an end so abruptly was too much to handle. Tim and I sat at the end of our bed and quoted **Psalm 23**. When I got to the verse, ***"Yea tho I walk through the valley of the shadow of death, I will fear no evil, for Thou art with me,"*** I knew that God would be with me even in this unspeakable event. It was without a doubt the worst day of my life, and somehow, I knew God would be there and take care of us.

We didn't sleep at all that night, and as the sun began to rise the next morning, I remember God gently whispering to me, "I made another day just for you. Live in it for me." And so, I did. With a heart broken in pieces and not knowing what to do next and how to live without my son, I woke up each day hoping and believing that God would not let me go. God told me that He was still in control and asked me to step out and believe Him. I didn't understand this. Brandon was my whole life. He knew me better than even my husband at that time. He could tell when I needed to talk, then come up to me, hug me and say, "Do you wanna talk?" Man, I want Brandon back! Why Brandon? Brandon was the reason I stayed alive when my first husband left me. Now he's not here! Nothing will ever be the same again. What is my new normal? How can I live? I feel so empty inside. One giant hole is now occupying my life. How could I ever watch our sports teams again without him? How am I going to make it through the holidays without my son? I will never see him get married, and I will never have grandchildren of my blood. Oh God, I can't do this. HELP! These were the questions I screamed out of my heart. They were the emptiness I felt. They were real feelings, and I wasn't sure I could survive.

That week Tim and I made arrangements with our Pastor that we thought we'd never have to make. We contacted a funeral home, started to organize a memorial service, wrote an obituary, and made burial decisions for our child. We ran on, "Gotta get this done; so don't feel, just do." We blocked out our emotions so the details of that week could be scheduled. The real "new normal" began after the memorial service and burial were done, and everyone left to get back to their lives. I'm not saying that everyone forgot about Brandon, but they had to get back to work and their reality while Tim and I felt abandoned. We were all alone to figure out what to do next with the house, Brandon's room, and how to pull me out of bed every morning. It was a task we weren't sure how to accomplish.

It took five years for the criminal court and civil courts to be completed. It wasn't until after all the courts were settled that Tim and I began the road of healing from this great-organized mess of losing our son. One thing I know for sure is that over the years, we finally received our joy. This joy rose to the surface as we talked about Brandon and even laughed a little when we remembered the crazy things Brandon would say or do. This was our joy. We finally felt comfort and peace after our great loss.

MATTHEW 5:4

God blesses those who mourn, for they will be comforted.

> **Be-IN-Couraged and know that even through your great loss, God is still there and loves you. He will comfort you in your time of need.**

LIFE WITHOUT BRANDON
REST IN GOD'S HANDS

There have been situations when I've felt such an intensity to seek God's face. Other times I've felt like I've needed to put my trust in God and have faith that He will answer my prayers in His time. This was one of those times. Brandon's death left me feeling empty, vulnerable, broken, and alone. There was an inevitable hole in my heart that I couldn't imagine ever being filled again. Where was God? Where was my trust in God?

This emptiness followed for months, but all the while I knew I wasn't alone. My faithful husband felt the same way yet we both knew that God was with us. We both knew that we had to rest in His hands until God decided that we were ready to move into a new way of living. What does that look like? This was our mission. We kept each other accountable in prayer and love during this most difficult time of our lives.

Mother Teresa once said, "Prayer is putting oneself in the hands of God." I believe that when we make our petitions known to God, we can rest in the fact that He knows what is best for us, and we can rest in Him waiting patiently for the answers. This, however, doesn't come naturally nor is it easy to do. It takes practice, and this horrible event of losing our child was put in front of us to practice placing our petitions and prayers in God's hands, and then rest — knowing that God hears us and will answer in His way and in His time.

ORGANIZED MESS

Could it be that this is one of those times for you to let God hold you and your prayers in His hands? Wait patiently for the answers. He will assuredly answer them in His sovereign time. Rest in God's hands.

PSALM 37:7

Rest in the Lord and wait patiently for Him; Do not fret because of him who prospers in his way, because of the man who brings wicked schemes to pass.

> **Be-IN-Couraged and know that God knows what you're going through. He will take care of you. Rest in the Lord and wait patiently for Him.**

LIFE WITHOUT BRANDON
THE LORD IS NEAR

We're not promised to have a life without worries or conflicts, but God does give us the promise of being present during our brokenness. He will give us joy, peace, comfort, and hope when we need it most.

God can do far beyond what we ask or imagine. Our job is to go to Him trusting that He is there. Discouragement keeps us from getting our prayers answered the way we want them answered. Lord help our unbelief! Trusting God in the dark times is where you will start to see God at work. I've had to trust God in my darkest hour of losing my son by a drunk driver. To me, this was the biggest test of my faith for trusting that God is still there even in my darkness. I had to trust and wait for His intervention of peace, comfort, hope, and even revived joy.

I've had broken relationships, a broken body, and a broken heart, but I know that God heals all of those areas. Do you need healing for a relationship or a broken heart? Go to God in prayer and tell Him how you feel. He is close to you and is hoping that you desire Him to deliver you from these broken areas in which you suffer. Trust God in your darkest hour and allow Him to do His work in your life, a work of healing and restoring.

ORGANIZED MESS

PSALM 34:18-19

The Lord is near to those who have a broken heart. Many are the afflictions of the righteous, but the Lord delivers him out of them all.

Be-IN-Couraged knowing that God is present and near to you during your times of struggle. Seek His joy, peace, comfort, and hope today.

LIFE WITHOUT BRANDON
HAVE YOU PRAYED ABOUT IT?

As a little girl, my mother would tell me stories of how her mom would disappear every day. No one in the family would worry about her because they knew she was praying deep in their backwoods. I never met my grandmother, but I know that she was a godly woman.

Every time I came to a crossroads, even as a young child, my mom would gently remind me to pray. At the age of seven, I was asked to go to two different friend's houses for dinner on the same night. I remember asking my mother which friend's house I should go to for dinner that particular night. She looked at me with a slightly silly grin on her face and said, "Have you prayed about it?" That's not what I wanted to hear! Why can't she just make it easy and tell me the right thing to do? She knew I'd ultimately make the right decision, but she wanted me to rely on God's decision, not hers or mine. I also brought up my son, Brandon, to pray. I taught him that prayer is the bridge to God for everything! He would frequently ask me about decisions on jobs, friends, etc. You got it; I would look him in the eyes and ask him that most familiar question, "Have you prayed about it?"

It was at his memorial service that I heard those wonderful words in a story from one of Brandon's friends. She spoke of conversations with Brandon on many occasions, but one, in particular, stood out to her. She had to make a big decision regarding something that was coming up in her life. Brandon's response to

ORGANIZED MESS

her was, "Have you prayed about it?" Evidently, he had that same silly grin on his face that my mother had on her face and that I had on my face when speaking those infamous words.

Yes, it's that simple. Yes, it works. Why is it that we try to figure things out on our own when all we have to do is ask God? He is willing and able to guide us in the decision-making process if we would only ask. Don't leave God out of your everyday decisions. And so, I ask you, have you prayed about it?

PROVERBS 3:5-6

Trust in the Lord with all your heart and lean not to your own understanding. In all your ways acknowledge Him, and He will direct your paths.

Be-IN-Couraged and pray about everything!

LIFE WITHOUT BRANDON
IN HIS PRESENCE

When Brandon died, all I could say was how much I needed strength to get me out of bed, take a shower, go to work, and try to get something done every day. It was a struggle, and I felt weak, emotionally and physically. The twenty-third Psalm gave me an element of comfort, but I needed more than just God being with me through this valley. I needed His strength to get me through another sunrise and sunset. This was a task that I couldn't do on my own. My husband and I both needed strength from above, and we relied on each other's encouragement to seek God for this gift.

All right, so I knew what I needed, but how do I get there? I prayed that His strength would come sooner than later. Then I read **Nehemiah 8:10** that says **"Do not sorrow, for the joy of the Lord is your strength."** Laughter immediately rose up. It wasn't laughter of joy, but more like mocking laughter. Are you kidding me, God? Really? Is joy the answer to me gaining strength? Do you really think that I can have joy when the most important person in my life was abruptly taken from me? About a week later, I came back to the Lord with one question. If you plan to give me strength by giving me joy, how do I get this kind of deep, satisfying joy that I need?

This was becoming a puzzle, and I was getting frustrated looking for the missing pieces. I thought I just needed strength, but God knew that before strength I needed joy. Now I had to figure out how to get joy and strength.

A few years after seeking strength and joy, a friend called me out of the blue and gave me a scripture found in **Psalm 16:11**. It says, **"In your presence is fullness of joy."** That's it! The Lord knew when to give me this missing piece of the puzzle, and He showed me that it was all about being in His presence. I couldn't make joy happen. If I did, it was temporary, and I already found that kind of joy in my home, job, car, and other things in life. That joy quickly ran dry, but the fullness of joy can only come from the Lord. I knew my next path in life would be one of getting back to prayer and spending time with God. In doing this, He promised me the joy I needed to ultimately gain His strength and get through another day.

Over a period of time, God's fullness of joy did give me strength. It worked. I spent more time with God, and He gave me what I really needed. I got more than what I initially asked for. I got joy, strength, and a close relationship with God. This relationship has increased as I continued to spend each day in His presence. Now I talk with God all the time. We laugh together and cry together. It's wonderful, and I wouldn't change it for any other kind of joy or strength that I could get elsewhere. With or without my son here on earth, I have joy. I have strength. And it's all because of Jesus!

Are you missing a piece of your puzzle? Could it be strength or joy? If so, spend time talking with God. He will get you through your day and your deepest hurt. God promises to be with us and give us what we need. Seek His face, and you will get what He knows you need!

PSALM 23:1-4

The Lord is my shepherd, I shall not want. He makes me lie down in green pastures, he leads me beside still waters, he restores my soul. He guides me in paths of righteousness for his name's sake. Even though I walk through the valley of the shadow of death, I will fear no evil, for you are with me.

NEHEMIAH 8:10

Do not sorrow, for the joy of the Lord is your strength.

PSALM 16:11

In your presence is fullness of joy.

> **Be-IN-Couraged! If you seek missing pieces to your puzzle of life, seek the Lord instead and watch Him fulfill your every need!**

LIFE WITHOUT BRANDON
MY ROLE MODEL

Who is your role model? Who inspires you to be better than you are today? Who is the one person who gives and gives, and never asks for anything back? These questions are easy for me to answer. I've learned many lessons over the years; lessons of grace, mercy, love, and kindness. A role model is described as a person looked to by others as an example to be imitated. The obvious answer to my, "Who is your role model?" question would be Jesus. Of course, He is our role model to follow, but I also have another role model that I've admired. That would be my son, Brandon. I've learned so much from Brandon who had no idea the impact he made in my life. He taught me how to be loving, kind, and how to put others before myself. How can such a young person be so impactful on someone who is twenty-one years older than he?

Just before Brandon was born, I remember thinking, "How is it possible to love someone so much when you've never met him?" He was my pride and joy, and my heart was full just watching him grow into the man that God created him to be. Now I need to stop you before you think he was this amazingly perfect specimen of a person. He was not. He was no angel, and yes, he made plenty of mistakes, but there were great qualities that rose up as he grew up. He wanted to be a good person, and He loved Jesus more than anyone else.

Brandon had boundaries, and he set these boundaries so that he wouldn't fall into the plot of the enemy. There were many times when I had to remind him that his attitude needed an adjustment. It would often fall on the aftermath of listening to music or watching movies that were not positive. He would snap at me or be disrespectful, and I would say to him, "I think you need a TUDE adjustment!" Eventually, he knew that he was in the wrong, and he made adjustments to his lifestyle that would be pleasing to God.

I hope that my values, love, and kindness are half of what Brandon displayed. If that's the case, then I smile and continue to live for Jesus, as He desires. What else is there? So I ask again, who is your role model? Take a few minutes to think of this and wonder what it would look like if you would reflect the image of your role model. Then be that role model for someone else.

I THESSALONIANS 4:1

Finally, then we urge you in the name of the Lord Jesus to live in a way that pleases God, as we have taught you. You live this way already, and we encourage you to do so even more.

Be-IN-Couraged! Be that role model for someone else today. Walk in the way that God desires and seek to follow His ways.

MORE UNWELCOME LOSS

MORE UNWELCOME LOSS
REJECTION

I've been very familiar, and unfortunately closer than I'd like, with rejection. "Rejection" was my best friend for years. Rejection controlled me. I believed in rejection as if that was the normal way of life. Rejection stared me in the eyes when I was in fifth grade. My closest friend at the time turned her back on me to hang out with the "cool kids." She went from caring about me to making fun of me.

The next major encounter with rejection was when I was seventeen and in a serious relationship with my then boyfriend. We had talked about getting married, and then out of the blue he broke up with me to date a "cool cheerleader." I began a downward spiral fall that ended up in depression. I didn't see it at the time, but I know that God was with me through that difficult part of my life, and He wanted me to know that I was good enough for Him. He created me as His beautiful daughter, and it hurt His heart that mine was hurting so deeply. I just wanted to be loved, and I neglected to go to God first.

My life continued clinging to rejection as my companion. I got married when I was twenty and had a baby just before my twenty-third birthday. My husband at the time had a mysterious side that I was unfortunately attracted to. He began to stay out late after work with his co-workers, and one thing led to another. Before I knew it, he had an affair, and by the time my son turned two, he walked out the door.

He no longer wanted to be tied down to a wife and a son, so he said.

If these rejections weren't enough, my father told me in a phone conversation that he never loved my mother or his three girls. The whole idea of not being good enough flooded my mind once again. I could go on and on with stories of rejection in my life, but that's not where I want this to go. The fact was, I allowed rejection to control me over and over again and I was ready to stop that roller coaster ride. I was ready to go to God where I finally said "enough!"

I cried out to God asking Him to show me the kind of love only He could give. I was tired of being rejected by people, and just wanted someone to tell me that I was indeed good enough! Peace and comfort began to flood my mind, and the reality of finding out that I was good enough for God became overwhelming! God made me good enough, and He continues to drive that message home to me every day of my life.

Are you tired of being strangled by rejection? I encourage you to spend time in the presence of God and ask Him to fill you with His love. Give Him your mistakes, and your rejections. Allow His love to heal those areas in you that have controlled and paralyzed your life. This is a new day; a day to start believing that you are good enough and that you are loved by the God of creation. You are wonderfully made. All you have to do now is to believe it!

ORGANIZED MESS

PSALM 139:14

I will praise You, for I am fearfully and wonderfully made; Marvelous are Your works.

> **Be-IN-Couraged knowing that God says you're good enough!**

MORE UNWELCOME LOSS
LONELINESS

Along with the rejection in my life, came loneliness. The great valley of loneliness followed me for many years. I could be around those that I would call my friends, and yet I would be incredibly lonely. I became crippled with loneliness. I was hurting so deeply and felt like no one heard me screaming for help.

Prayer changed this behavior — Prayers from my Mom and others who saw how I was sinking. I turned to alcohol and other people to give me what I was lacking. I was looking for happiness, but nothing was filling the void. I knew God at that time but didn't have a daily relationship with Him. I only talked to Him occasionally. But Mom? She talked with God every day — all day long. She cried out to God, and He answered her prayers. Do you believe in the power of prayer? I sure do! I know without a shadow of a doubt that God is alive. He is always with me even during those times I don't "feel" Him.

I began to talk with and allow God to speak to me. This took time, but I can assuredly say that my loneliness eventually turned to joy — complete joy in the Lord. My fears of never being loved were put to death. God also brought me a man who loved God and me too. We grew together with God being in the middle . . . the innermost center of our lives and now the center of our marriage. God has reinforced the importance of spending time with Him and hearing His voice. I know that God is with me every day — all day long no matter what comes my way. He has my back, and He has yours too. His joy is in His children. He is there during our sorrows, our fears, and our laughter and joy. He is there to guide us and to lead us. He is the light in our pathway and will always love us unconditionally.

I said goodbye to loneliness a long time ago, and with God's help, I don't ever want to turn back.

ISAIAH 41:10

Fear not, for I am with you; Be not dismayed, for I am your God. I will strengthen you, Yes, I will help you, I will uphold you with My righteous right hand.

> **Be-IN-Couraged! Start talking to God and give Him your loneliness. He will assuredly turn your sorrow into joy!**

MORE UNWELCOME LOSS
MY YORKSHIRE TERRIER

I was so happy to get the most adorable puppy for my 40th birthday. To be honest with you, I never wanted a dog. I was more of a cat lover until my 40th birthday when I got my little Dale the Intimidator Sherman . . . my Yorkie. He certainly was not intimidating, but I loved NASCAR and watched Dale Earnhardt, Sr. race for many years, and he had the nickname of The Intimidator. I liked that, and therefore I ended up with my Yorkshire Terrier's name.

My little Dale was only two years old when Brandon died. He became very protective of me, in particular, from the moment the detective came to our front door and gave us the news of Brandon. I fell apart with screams of loss, and from that point on, Dale wouldn't let anyone hurt me. Funny, since Dale was only five pounds. He stuck to my side like glue. He did anything I asked of him, which included about 12 tricks. He was the smartest AKC dog I knew.

In June 2014 I noticed that Dale began to limp and even fell as he tripped over his hind feet. This began with one leg and followed by the other hind leg. By the end of the next day, Dale's front legs went paralyzed along with his hind legs. We took him to the vet and got blood work done, and the report came back the next day showing that Dale's protein levels were higher than normal. The vet said this meant there was something wrong with his body, but they didn't know exactly what it was. They put my little five-pound dog on antibiotics and steroids, but by the end of the third day, his whole body was paralyzed.

At this point, I knew that he wasn't going to make it. I had prayed for healing in Dale's little body, but I also had to give him to God. I knew that Dale's days and even hours were numbered, and all I wanted to do was hold him the rest of the day. I whispered in his ears, "It's ok." Dale went in and out of consciousness, and in the wee-hours of the fourth day, Dale passed away. Once again, I was devastated. Dale was only thirteen, and I wasn't sure how I'd survive without my precious puppy.

One thing I have learned through this loss is that God cares about everything in my life. He cares about every detail of my life, and yes even our animals who mean so much to us. Dale was given to me for a reason. He helped me get through the toughest time of my life — losing my son, and Dale was there for the happy times. He studied me and knew when I was happy and when I needed him to snuggle. He was my companion and loved me unconditionally.

God knows what we need, and sometimes gives us a dog or another animal to help us walk in this life. I find refuge in knowing that God cares about everything.

PSALM 46:1

God is our refuge and strength, a very present help in times of trouble.

Be-IN-Couraged knowing that God cares about everything in our lives — even our animals.

MORE UNWELCOME LOSS
MY DAD

As a child, I grew up in a household where I thought that my dad was the "normal" kind of dad. That couldn't be farther from the truth. Or was it? What exactly is normal anyways? I'm not completely sure, but I know that my fairytale dad didn't exist. He rarely, if ever, hugged me and told me how much he loved his daughter. My dad brought laughter to our family, we enjoyed stock car racing together, but he wasn't one to give much emotional support.

After 37 years of my parent's marriage, my dad left my mother for another woman. Now I'm not saying that it was all one-sided. I'd be foolish to think that, but my heart broke for my mom who was now in a vulnerable situation. My two sisters and I were all adults in our thirties at that time, and we were all married with children. Mom was left alone. The feelings of my divorce came flooding back into my mind, and I wanted to help the one woman who was there for me my whole life. I lived 3000 miles away so I couldn't see her, but would call her often, and pray for her all the time. That's what she did all those years for me, and that's what I felt I could give her during her disastrous time. Prayer is underrated and taken for granted by so many people. But in my house, it's non-negotiable. Prayer is a must for any relationship to work.

When I asked my dad what happened and why he left, he explained to me that he never loved my mother nor did he create the three of us girls out of love. I asked him if he loved his daughters now, and he simply didn't reply. His silence was deafening! This was so devastating and became an eye-opening reality of my dad's existence for me. As I pondered my life prior to that moment, I realized that there weren't many moments that he embraced me or played with me when I was very young. Again, I just thought this was normal.

At that horrible moment of truth, I saw my loss. I felt a huge hole in my heart. Was it any wonder that the man in my first marriage was just like my dad who ran off with another woman? I ran towards the only thing I knew at that time, but God, once again, had a different plan for me.

It was odd, but the more I prayed for my dad, the more joy I felt. Nothing apparently had changed in my dad from the outside, yet joy filled my heart. No matter what was said, I knew that my mission was to pray for dad every day. It was a difficult task, but over the next several years I saw a change in my dad's spiritual heart as his physical body was failing. I had peace from the Lord that everything was going to be all right. It was my job to pray and leave the results to God who knows all and can change people. I had to be fearless — the peace that comes from the Lord doesn't include fear, so I made an effort to trust in Him alone and just pray.

I realized that my sense of security must not rest in the things going our way. Sometimes God will use what we call bad situations and bring good out of them. My dad had three triple by-pass surgeries, and we all knew that his days were numbered. Dad spent so much time in and out of the hospital over several years, and God used that time and spoke to my dad in a personal way. I could only trust that God knew what He was doing in my dad's life.

Then I got the call. The call that said my dad passed away. I knew in my heart that I would see him again. I have great peace about him to this day. That was my joy in the midst of my loss. The joy that I'll see my dad again and this time he will love me unconditionally and wholly.

JOHN 14:27

Peace I leave with you; my peace I give you. I do not give to you as the world gives. Do not let your hearts be troubled and do not be afraid.

> **Be-IN-Couraged and know that your prayers never go unheard. Do your part and pray. Then leave the results to God who loves His children more than we can comprehend!**

MORE UNWELCOME LOSS
MY INSPIRING MOM

I'm sure you know by now that my Mom is one of the closest and most influential people in my life. She is my prayer warrior and has prayed for me my whole life. She is selfless, kind, and loving. Many people have called her "Mom" even though she has no blood relation to them. That's who she is. She would help others whenever she could. In fact, the Lord told her that she was His Helper. That is an amazing title, and it fully describes my Mom.

My wonderful Mom was diagnosed with Alzheimer's disease in the beginning of 2013. I had seen signs of this disease in her life since the death of my Dad in November 2010. I got all the Power of Attorney paperwork in order while she still had a clear mind, which I am very grateful for. What I didn't know at the time was how quickly Mom would go from knowing everything to not recognizing anyone — even her daughter.

I went to see Mom in January of 2015, and that's when God spoke to me. Over the past two years, I've been so consumed with taking care of my mother that I forgot to stop and really look at her. I took care of her social security paperwork, health insurance, and moving Mom from her apartment into a memory care facility. The list for taking care of my amazing mother was lengthy.

God reminded me of when I taught Brandon to stop, look and listen before he walked across the street. God had me stop and look at Mom that cool day in

January. She was eating her lunch, and I just watched. She always had a smile on her face no matter what. I saw an incredible peace within my mother. I knew this peace was from God. I saw no strife, no struggles, and no stress in her. This was because she had none of these. She was well taken care of and didn't have a worry in the world. She was at complete peace, which is the positive side of Alzheimer's.

I then began to thank God for what I saw and for the work He had done in Mom's life. Although I still believe that Alzheimer's is a horrible disease, I know that God has made something good and positive out of it. I hope this reminds us all to stop, look, and listen to what God is doing in every aspect of our lives.

I went to see Mom on Thanksgiving Day, 2015, and the unthinkable happened. She didn't know me. I left that visit with tears rolling down my face and was held in the embrace of my husband. It was a terribly difficult day for me. Mom has not known me since, but I know that she knows Jesus and that the Holy Spirit still dwells in her. This has become my hope and comfort, while Mom is still living on what we call Earth. I was reminded that when nothing else registers in Mom, she still knows and feels my love. When I didn't know what to do or what to say during a visit to Mom, I was told, "just love her." Jesus' love is relentless, non-stopping, never-ending, and persistent!

When nothing else registers for us, we need to remember the love of Jesus and His relentless non-stopping, never-ending, persistent love. We all want and need this love. We also need to share this kind of love with others. When you're faced with a difficult person, you don't need to say anything. Just love them!

ORGANIZED MESS

Mom's health has been up and down since 2015. I know that one day I will get the dreaded call letting me know she has passed away, but I will also rejoice on that day because she will have finally made her grand destination. She will be with Jesus and will be at complete peace — at last. Yes, it will be difficult, but I know that I will see my Mom again and she will be completely whole. We will rejoice on that blessed day!

HEBREWS 13:5
I will never leave you or forsake you.

I CORINTHIANS 13:13
Now abides faith, hope, love, these three; but the greatest of these is love!

> **Be-IN-Couraged and show someone love today! When all else fails, stop, look, listen, and just love them!**

MORE UNWELCOME LOSS
UNEXPECTED LIFE JOURNEYS

Just when we think we're safe and everything is going well, another unwelcome loss comes into view. Life is full of unexpected occurrences, which is why our trust has to be in the Lord. These occurrences or journeys test our trust in the Lord. Let me explain. There was a time when I had no job and was about to lose our home. Also, I had always been involved with worship teams at every church I'd been in since I was a teenager, and now I found myself not having the outlet that gave me such joy. I felt destitute and wasn't sure where I fit. I had been stripped of so much, yet I knew God was still in control.

After my Mom asked her church group to pray that a job would open up for me, a woman from that group came up to me one Sunday and asked if I would consider a job involving music. I'd have to drive thirty-five minutes each day to work, but she had a strong feeling that God led her to me. I took down the information, and after talking with my husband; I proceeded to call about the job the following morning. I had been praying for weeks, and I had peace about this particular job. I found myself in an interview two days later and started working two weeks after that. God intervened in a way that I couldn't see. He knew the beginning from the end, and He had specific intentions of supplying all of our needs. Tim's work increased, I got a full-time job, and I was able to enjoy the worship that took place at my job. Because of this job, God also supplied our home. God is good, and I know that He was the one to make all this possible.

I've learned that these unexpected life journeys can be lessons learned of God's grace and mercy if we continue to keep our focus on Him. Keep our eyes on God, not our circumstances. Our circumstances will only drag us down and bring depression, but God gives us hope, joy, and light at the end of the tunnel. He is our provider. God can do exceedingly abundantly more than what we ask or even think. I know now that should I accept the challenge, the unexpected life journeys I face will have a greater ending than it's beginning.

Are you in a place where you feel destitute and running on empty? Don't stop praying! Keep trusting in God to meet your needs. He will do more than you can expect and will show you His grace and mercy through your journey.

EPHESIANS 3:20

Now to Him who is able to do exceedingly abundantly above all that we ask or think, according to the power that works in us.

> **Be-IN-Couraged and know that God is in control even if it doesn't look like it. Keep trusting in Him and accept His grace and mercy during your unexpected life journeys.**

LIFE NOW WITH ENCOURAGEMENT

LIFE NOW WITH ENCOURAGEMENT
SCARS FROM OUR UNWELCOME LOSS

About thirty years ago I had arthroscopic knee surgery. My knee was painful, and I had no choice but to go through with the planned surgery. My Mom prayed with me just before I went into surgery, and when everything was done, the doctor came in looking a bit puzzled. My Mom asked him what was wrong, and he said, "Well that's the thing. Nothing was wrong. Jan's knee is 100% ok. We looked around several times to see what needed to be cleaned out so Jan could heal, and there was nothing wrong!"

My Mom immediately burst out saying, "Thank you, Lord!" God answered our prayers! From that point on, I've never had a problem or pain in my knee. God healed my body, and I was so grateful. However, I've often wondered why I had to endure the surgery if God intended to heal me all along. Maybe the doctor needed to hear that God ultimately was the healer? I don't know that answer, but now I have four little scars to remind me that God indeed heals today!

Our scars always remind us of something we've been through. Maybe that reminder is physical. Maybe it's not a great memory, but it's our story. Our oldest son had a three-wheeler accident when he was about thirteen years old, and it's left a nasty burn scar on his arm. However, he liked that scar when he was a teenager because he had a story to tell, and the girls loved it! That was his story, and he was proud of it.

Do you have scars that tell a story? Are those scars physical or maybe emotional? My prayer is that we all can turn our emotional scars from pain to joy. But how? Maybe you have a scar from an unwelcome loss, and you want to do everything except remember how it got there. Sometimes we don't see the hand of God in our lives until years after the scar has appeared. Sometimes it takes a long time to see how God has replaced our sorrow with His joy. All my scars were not happy ones. The emotional scars of losing Brandon at age nineteen were devastating, but several years later I saw how Brandon's life had touched others and how it still gives them joy and hope. This gives me comfort.

Always remember that Jesus endured scars for us and that His scars remind us of how much He loved us. Everything that I write in this book is to encourage you and remind you that if you choose, your hope can be in the Lord. He can be the one to give you unspeakable joy. He can be the one who turns your sorrow into joy. Thank the Lord for your scars, and please tell your story to encourage someone else today!

PSALM 30:5

Weeping may endure for a night, but joy comes in the morning!

Be-IN-Couraged and know that although we have scars, they can be a reminder that God heals and that He can turn our sorrow into joy.

LIFE NOW WITH ENCOURAGEMENT
A HEART OF GRATITUDE

My husband and I have two little Yorkshire Terriers and we love to walk them in the mornings. One day while I was walking my dog I stopped to hear the birds sing. There must have been ten birds singing at the top of their little lungs. It was a wonderful symphony of chirps!

I noticed that there was one bird in particular who had a very loud chirp. I thought this bird must be large to make such a glorious sound! However, when I got closer to the sound, I saw that it was a very tiny bird. Now I'm not a bird person per say, so I don't know what kind of bird this was, but it's as though this little bird wanted everyone to hear him and his heart of gratitude. Then I thought, how amazing would it be if we raised our voices loudly with a heart of gratitude to our creator?

I walked away that morning with a purpose in my heart to be more grateful to God for everything I had. I made that day my day of gratitude. Sometimes we've been thrown a curve ball and say, "I didn't see that coming!" Even in those not-so-good days, we can find something good — something we can give thanks back to God. I even put a sticky note on my desktop computer that says "Have a Heart of Gratitude." The birds have it so why shouldn't I?

There's great refreshment in the Lord when we have a heart of gratitude. But what if you can't seem to find anything to be grateful for? I say, (with a smile on my face) "go camping!" One summer while camping, my husband and I sat at the campfire and listened to the crickets sing in unison. It was exactly what we needed after weeks of stress and illness with our family. The first day at our campsite we listened to the downpour of rain and the crack of thunder. The majesty of God's presence lingered in the billions of stars at night. All of this brought us to that heart of gratitude. There was no better place to bring a prayer of thanksgiving for everything I was experiencing. When we got back home, we were once again reminded that this same heart of gratitude could be our daily occurrence. I could actually be refreshed at home, at work, or on a camping trip. It's up to me to see and hear what God is doing around me at every moment.

The Lord asks us to be thankful in all things. That certainly isn't easy, and although I've been through a lot in my life, I owe it all to God for my existence today. The Apostle Paul said to give thanks to God for everything (Ephesians 5:20). Think of it. Always giving thanks for everything — no matter the circumstance! Nothing turns us into bitter, selfish, dissatisfied people more quickly than an ungrateful heart. And nothing will do more to restore contentment and joy than a thankful heart.

Can you have a thankful heart towards God where you are right now? Thank God for material blessings that He has given you. Thank God for the people in your life. Thank God in the middle of your crisis. Thank God especially for His salvation in Jesus Christ and thank God for His continued presence and power in your life. Sing in your heart like the birds. Sing loudly to the Lord. Take the time right now to be refreshed with a heart of gratitude.

EPHESIANS 5:19-20

Sing and make music in your heart to the Lord, always giving thanks to God the Father for everything.

I THESSALONIANS 5:16-18

Be joyful always; pray continually; give thanks in all circumstances, for this is God's will for you in Christ Jesus.

> **Be-IN-Couraged! I challenge you to make this day your "Day of Gratitude" even if things don't go as planned.**

LIFE NOW WITH ENCOURAGEMENT
STAY IN HIS PRESENCE

One spring morning I took a walk in my neighborhood and came near some orange trees that had tons of blossoms. I just had to stop and smell the blossoms! They were intoxicating, and before I knew it my whole face was smothered in a branch that had multiple blossoms. Being careful not to get stung by the bees who were also enjoying the beautiful scent, I slowly pulled back, but lingered in the fragrance of what I call the most beautiful Spring flower! The scent was intensifying as I continued to surround myself in the midst of these trees. I didn't want to leave, even though time was haunting me to do my ever-so-important errands of that day.

Then I thought of how I approach God. Do I run through my prayers just to check it off my list and not notice how beautiful that place of prayer is? Do I continue to stay and smother my life with prayer because God's presence is so intoxicating that I don't want to leave? Are there bees around my area of prayer that causes me to pull away, so I don't stay in the presence of God? I realized that this was my choice. I could leave the presence of God or choose to stay in His presence.

There is peace and comfort in the Lord's presence, and when I go face-to-face with difficulties, I have to stop and spend time with God. Sometimes it's simply being still — not saying a word. These are the times I find great peace and comfort. These are the times I treasure and ultimately hear from God. He is my constant companion, and He brings lightness to my steps. He is my burden-bearer with all my unresolved issues that weigh me down. We can't get away from trials and distress, but we don't have to let them control us and get us down! Staying in His presence is the answer to my stressful situations. I'm reminded to keep my focus on God and let today's plans and problems start to leave my mind.

That Spring morning, I broke off a branch of orange blossoms and brought it home to remind me to stay in the presence of God more and enjoy just being with Him. I don't want the bees or other distractions to pull me away from where I know I need to linger. What about you? Are you running through the beauty of being in God's presence or will you choose to stay with purpose and soak in His beauty? I hope your choice is to stay in His presence and experience what He has for you this day.

PSALM 105:4

Look to the Lord and his strength; seek his face always.

Be-IN-Couraged! Stay in the Lord's presence where you will find rest, peace, comfort, and joy for your day!

LIFE NOW WITH ENCOURAGEMENT
LAUGH OFTEN

Laughter is good for the soul. The Bible affirms the healing power of joy when it says in **Proverbs 17:22, "A merry heart does good like medicine, but a broken spirit dries the bones."** This scriptural truth suggests that laughter holds as much healing power as medicine. Is it any wonder that those who laugh easily often live longer than those who do not?

I visited my Mom recently, and we laughed together — for no good reason. Or was it for every good reason? You see, my Mom doesn't speak nor does she know me at this point in her life. So, for my Mom to laugh out loud with nothing said was a wonderful experience! I laughed with her. At that moment, I realized that I take things way too seriously. I was reminded that day to lighten up a bit and laugh more.

Can you think of the last time you broke out in laughter for no reason? Maybe it's time to do just that. There are times that I have to purposefully think of something that makes me laugh, like my son doing the craziest of things or a child's giggle. The other day my dog burped really loud, and my husband and I looked at each other and started laughing. It was wonderful!

Laughter lightens the load of life's seriousness and brings back the joy that is missing. Children have a way of doing this seamlessly. They don't think about it. They don't have a lot on their plates to make them serious. They love everyone. They can forget about a fight they just had five minutes ago with their sibling and play, laugh, and love like nothing ever happened. Why is it that they can laugh, love, and have fun a lot more than me? Maybe the point here is that I need to be more like a child — laugh often and love always! Can you relate to that?

PROVERBS 15:13

A merry heart makes a cheerful countenance, but by sorrow of the heart, the spirit is broken.

Be-IN-Couraged and laugh often!

LIFE NOW WITH ENCOURAGEMENT
GOD IS GOOD!

Those that know me know that I often say, "GOD IS GOOD." I say it a lot because I truly believe that God is good! Maybe you've heard people say back and forth, "God is good . . . All the time . . . And all the time . . . God is good!" It's easy to say that God is good when everything is going great, and you have no problems. But what about the times when a monkey wrench has been thrown into your otherwise carefully planned out day? What then? Is God still good during those times of fear, anxiety, stress, loneliness, and unwelcome loss?

When you are faced with difficult situations and stress rises to the top, it may not be that easy to mutter those words. What about times when a family member has cancer? Is God still good then? When a loved one passes away, do you see the goodness of God then? Or what about when you've lost your closest pet or are in the middle of a difficult divorce? Is God still good when you've lost your job, and you don't have the finances to pay the utilities or the mortgage? The answer to all of these is YES! God is good in everything. I realize that sometimes it's harder to see that God is good when you are going through hardships, but when you're on the other side of your sorrow or strife, you will ultimately see how good God was and still is today.

God never changes. He is the same yesterday, today, and tomorrow, and He is good in everything we face. It's our lives that change, not God. God wants us closer to Him in our everyday lives, whether good or bad. I gain peace in the middle of my storms by saying those three little words: GOD IS GOOD! There's peace that cannot be explained because sometimes nothing has changed about my circumstances. But God is at work, and He is constantly changing me!

I want to encourage you to say, "God is good," over and over. Why? Because God is still good even when unwelcome loss sneaks into our lives. He is our only constant, and He will be there every step of the way. Repeat those three little words until you believe it. Then see what happens. It'll change your life!

HEBREWS 13:8
Jesus Christ is the same yesterday and today and forever.

Be-IN-Couraged and say "GOD IS GOOD" every day, and often.

LIFE NOW WITH ENCOURAGEMENT
YOU ARE GOOD ENOUGH!

As I've previously written, I went through many years of believing that I would never be good enough. Not good enough for a great job. Not enough for my Dad, not good enough for my friends and husband, and certainly not good enough for God's love. I was seeking approval from everyone but God. All I wanted was to have friends and family think I was good enough for them to invest their time and love in me. I used to say and do things that I believed they wanted me to say and do, and the day came where I didn't even know whom I was or what I liked to do.

As humans, we often seek the approval of so many people like our boss, our parents, and our friends. In my eyes, I was never good enough and ended up a very lonely person. Our young girls are told they are too fat, too skinny, or their face is ugly. These figurative portraits of girls have put dampers on their self-esteem.

What if we saw ourselves through the eyes of a blind person? What would we see then? One thing for sure is that we wouldn't see the outer skin at all. We would see what we were made of underneath our skin. This is how God sees us. He looks beyond the outward appearance and finds joy in His creation. He said that we are wonderfully made. He also has many loving thoughts toward us. In fact, they are never-ending. Just like the sandy shoreline, each grain of sand is like a loving thought from God towards His children. They are too numerous to count!

ORGANIZED MESS

God created us and loves us just the way we are. We may think that we're not good enough, not pretty enough, and not loved, but God says that we ARE good enough. We are beautiful and perfect just the way He made us. And most importantly God says we are loved!

I eventually stopped seeking the approval of everyone and started seeking God's approval. He is the one that loves me more than anyone. I hope that you can stop trying to seek the approval of others because you are good enough in the eyes of the Lord! Now it's up to you to believe it!

PSALM 139:17-18

How precious to me are your thoughts, O God! How vast is the sum of them! If I would count them, they are more than the sand.

> **Be-IN-Couraged knowing that God loves you just the way you are!**

LIFE NOW WITH ENCOURAGEMENT
THERE IS A SEASON

Webster's Dictionary describes grief or sorrow as "To worry; mental suffering caused by loss, disappointment, sadness, or affliction." Grief is intense emotional suffering caused by loss, hardship, or deep sadness. The Bible tells us that as sorrowful as we can get, we can always be rejoicing.

Over many years of grief, I've learned that there are seasons in our lives. Just as the seasons of our calendar, Winter, Summer, Spring, and Fall, there are seasons in our lives. Ecclesiastes chapter three explains that there is a season for everything and a time to every purpose under the heaven. I know that just as there is a time of sorrow, there will be a time of laughter. How long these times last is unknown and a great mystery, but I know that laughter will surely arrive.

Jesus had grief too. We are to be like Him in all areas, so we are also to have grief in our lives. Isaiah 53:4 speaks of Jesus taking our grief and our sorrows. So, my thought is if He is willing to take all of it, why keep any of it? I choose to give it up to Jesus and let His joy fill my life. You also have a choice. You can continue living with grief and sorrow or allow God's joy to fill the void in your life. It's up to you.

When my son's life was taken, I was sure that I'd never laugh again. In fact, I was convinced of it. I remember the first time I laughed, I immediately stopped and thought how horrible that was and yet how wonderful it felt. Brandon was full of laughter and would want us to laugh more and be less serious. Yes, over time my deep sorrow ended, and I was overcome with great joy. The joy of the Lord was revived, and I was ok.

II CORINTHIANS 6:10
As sorrowful, yet always rejoicing.

ECCLESIASTES 3:4
A time to weep, and a time to laugh; a time to mourn, and a time to dance;

> **Be-IN-Couraged! Give up your grief and sorrows to the Lord. He'll take them free of charge!**

LIFE NOW WITH ENCOURAGEMENT
HINDS' FEET ON HIGH PLACES

It was a beautiful summer day, and my husband and I decided to take our kayaks to the lake. We got there when it was early in the morning, and we were one of the first boats on the water. The lake was like glass without a ripple of a wave. As we paddled across the lake into the canyon, there wasn't a sound of another boat anywhere near us. The canyon walls were enormous, and the landscape was beautiful. What a great day to hear God's voice and see His creation!

As we paddled around a bend, we saw eight to ten bighorn sheep at the water's edge drinking the refreshing morning water. What a wonderful sight! My husband and I stopped paddling and let the kayaks rest on the quiet water as we continued to watch these amazing animals drink their morning water. As soon as they were done, they quickly turned around and leaped up the side of the canyon. In no time they had reached the highest ledge. It was an incredible sight! They leapt from ledge to ledge not even thinking how they would climb that enormous canyon wall.

It was at that moment that I remembered the scripture my mother gave me when I was a teenager. The strength that our Lord gives along with His grip on our lives allow us to climb the highest mountain as if we had hinds' feet. It was a teachable moment for me, and a great reminder of how much our God loves us. When we are hit with an unwelcome loss, God is there to train and teach us how to climb — without the thought of possibly slipping, because He is always with us to help us overcome what seems to be an impossible journey.

This is my joy. The joy from God who gives me the strength to endure the toughest of times and conquer whatever He has for me. He always meets me where I am and gently encourages me by giving me feet like hinds' feet.

HABAKKUK 3:19
The Lord God is my strength, and He will make my feet like hinds' feet, and He will make me to walk upon high places.

Be-IN-Couraged and know that God will go with you wherever you are, and He will make your feet sturdy to endure the rocky, rugged places in your life.

LIFE NOW WITH ENCOURAGEMENT
A LIFE WORTH WATCHING

Someone once asked me if one day my life flashed before my eyes, would it be worth watching? My first thought was, "NO — not a chance!" I've been through so much pain and suffering that, no, my life wouldn't be worth watching. However, even though I've had a lot of difficult times over my life and I've made some really stupid decisions, I've seen the hand of God in every aspect of every difficult time.

Even those times that I didn't go to God right away, I look back now and see how God has used that particular situation to guide me into a life He was preparing; a life worth watching.

He's still doing that today. He's preparing the way for me to go. He's guiding me on the path He has chosen for me. He has given me strength, joy, and His presence to be able to walk the path that He has prepared. What that path looks like is usually unknown to me. However, I am learning to put my trust in the One who knows my future.

Over my life, I've seen how God is with me and absolutely for me. His love is indescribable and undeniable. I've learned that suffering is a vital part of life. No one is exempt from suffering, and everyone can overcome the pain this life offers through Jesus. There are three things that I try to remember when going through pain and suffering:

ORGANIZED MESS

1. Stay close to God and remember that my suffering is temporary
2. Suffering does not define me, but it does create a life worth watching
3. Suffering gives the opportunity to produce joy

I am living proof that the Lord will bring you out of suffering if you let Him. I encourage you to allow God to mold you into who He desires you to become. You will see how you can gain strength and trust through times of trouble. Don't be discouraged, and never give up!

And so, I ask you if one day your life flashed before your eyes, would it be one worth watching? I hope your answer is emphatically, "YES."

ROMANS 8:31

If God is for us, who can be against us?

> **Be-IN-Couraged! Stay close to God and allow His love to overwhelm you so that one day you can say your life is worth watching.**

LIFE NOW WITH ENCOURAGEMENT
CHOICES

You may be asking how I got to where I am today? My simple, but very complex answer is the choices I've made. It's all about choices. We can choose to be negative and let our grief keep us down, or we can choose to look to God to pick us up and give us joy, which is the strength we need in order to endure to the end of our grief. Stop being negative and complaining. Focus on Jesus and who He is . . . not just on our circumstances. When I need a little extra strength to get through my unwelcome loss, I just ask for a little extra joy from the Lord. God promises us that our grief will turn into joy, so He must have an abundance of joy to give!

I also know that during my times of peace and laughter, I have to spend more time with God. I've realized how important this time is and it's one area of my life I don't want to compromise. If I don't already have fuel in my tank, then how can I run effectively when grief hits me between the eyes? I'm going nowhere without fuel from the Lord. My focus has to be on God and not the grief. This focus helps increase my trust in the Lord and furthermore builds a great foundation for the next season of grief.

None of us is exempt from grief. We all will face it at one time or another. But what I completely know and understand is that God is with me every time that grief hits. It's my choice that dictates how long I allow loss to hinder my walk. I started writing down what I call my, "Joy Moments." I wrote down everything that brought me joy. I add to this list often. Here are a few of my favorite Joy Moments:

Cool breeze at the ocean
Remembering Brandon's laughter and his silliness
The smell of rain hitting the hot pavement
When my dog snuggles with me
Hiking, kayaking, snowshoeing, biking, or camping
Noticing God's beautiful landscape
Flower and vegetable gardens
Clouds and rainy days
A baby's giggle

ROMANS 5:3-5

We can rejoice, too, when we run into problems and trials, for we know that they are good for us — they help us learn to be patient. And patience develops strength of character in us and helps us trust God more each time we use it until finally our hope and faith are strong and steady. Then, when that happens, we are able to hold our heads high no matter what happens and know that all is well, for we know how dearly God loves us, and we feel this warm love everywhere within us because God has given us the Holy Spirit to fill our hearts with his love.

JOHN 16:20

You will grieve, but your grief will turn to joy.

> **Be-IN-Couraged and choose to focus on God and not the sorrow that is before you. Start keeping a journal of your Joy Moments today.**

LIFE NOW WITH ENCOURAGEMENT
DON'T WORRY

I've spent way too many hours worrying about how I'm going to get through the loss I'm experiencing. I'm not sure why I worry so much. After all, I can't add an hour to my day or stop the tides from happening. God is the one who knows the beginning from the end, and if I could just trust in Him with all my heart, I most certainly wouldn't worry half as much as I do. I need to have purpose in my heart not to be anxious or fearful, but rather to trust in the Lord. This isn't easy, and it takes a lot of practice, but when the next trial hits, I'm a tiny bit quicker in giving it to the Lord without fear, anxiety, worry, or stress.

Thanking the Lord is another very important piece of not worrying. When I go through difficult situations, I'm learning to thank the Lord for something in my life or for those around me. This takes my mind off of what I'm going through and my focus back on God. There's always something to be thankful for even if it's just that I'm able to breathe, walk, and see the beauty of God's creation.

Sometimes I've got to stop and be still. Prayer is essential in my life of no worries and being still to hear the voice of God is crucial. I'm so accustomed to talk my head off and say amen before I even give God the chance to chime in on the conversation. I end up having one-way conversations and then close out my prayers to get going. But when I take the time to stop and wait on the Lord, it's a wonderfully peaceful time. I feel so much better even if I don't hear anything back. Sometimes when my problems get overwhelming, and I feel inadequate praying for myself, I start praying for other people. In these situations, praying for others is a good thing. It takes my mind off my problems, and I focus on other people. I love chai tea, and I love to pray, so to get things done, I often say, "Nothing that a cup of chai tea and prayer can't handle." I'm not exactly sure that a cup of chai really does anything, but I know that prayer does! Prayer is non-negotiable for me every day — all day.

Music has always been a relaxing thing for me. If I'm stressed and anxious over decisions or the craziness of life, I listen to music. Worshipping is getting close to the heart of God, and it gives me great joy. Once I start to worship with music, my heart and mind are centered in Christ, and I'm able to think more clearly.

Sometimes I've just got to call on a good friend or family member who is my "safe place." There are people in my life that I can go to at any time and just talk or ask for prayer. I encourage you to find that person or people who you trust and who can be your "safe place" to talk and pray together. We all need each other in so many ways, so I hope you have trust in someone close to you.

Whatever it is that helps you get from worry to the place of trusting in God; I hope that you practice it and that it gives you peace and comfort during your time of difficulty. One thing I know for sure, nothing is impossible with God. Our job is to let go of the worry and trust in Him, so He can show us the miracle only He can perform!

LUKE 12:25-26

Who of you by worrying can add a single hour to his life? Since you cannot do this very little thing, why do you worry about the rest?

LUKE 1:37

For nothing is impossible with God.

> **Be-IN-Couraged! Let go of your worry and begin to walk in faith by putting your trust in God through prayer and encouragement from others.**

LIFE NOW WITH ENCOURAGEMENT
FIND THE JOY IN EVERY ORGANIZED MESS

As long as we live on this great planet called Earth, we will inevitably come in contact with an unwelcome loss. How we react to our loss is the key to our outcome. If we react in a way that's pleasing to God and in a way that will grow our walk and relationship with Him, then we've done all right. Don't get me wrong. Our reactions can sometimes get emotional. I'm prone to cry a lot and get angry too, but when that happens, I try to ask God what it was that had triggered my emotions. Is there something I should be aware of in my life and this particular situation that has caused my emotions to go haywire? Or is it just time to spend with God in quiet prayer? It's a check and balance system that I have, and it's created a closer bond between me and my Heavenly Father who loves me so much. It may be a time just to get re-aligned with Christ and be reminded that He is the One who gives me the peace, joy, and comfort that I need.

Finding joy in the middle of a crisis is not easy, but deep inside of us is a joy unspeakable that has been put there by our creator. He is the living piece of the puzzle that I couldn't live without. Where would I be without God in my life? I most likely wouldn't be here today to speak words of encouragement to many who are down and discouraged. God has turned my ashes to joy, and I give Him praise!

I'm very thankful for the difficult days. I am the person I am today because of these difficult days, and

I wouldn't change any of those times. I know that prayer is important because it changes me! I don't like difficult times, but when they come, I know what I've got to do . . . pray and see how my life changes yet again, because of my relationship with the One who knows my tomorrow.

PROVERBS 31:25

She is clothed with strength and dignity; she can laugh at the days to come.

Be-IN-Couraged!

www.ingramcontent.com/pod-product-compliance
Lightning Source LLC
LaVergne TN
LVHW051525070426
835507LV00023B/3314